Change Management

IT Infrastructure Library

LONDON: THE STATIONERY OFFICE

Central Computer and Telecommunications Agency

For further information regarding this
publication and other CCTA products
please contact:
Library
CCTA
Roseberry Court
St Andrews Business Park
Norwich NR7 0HS
Tel. 01603 704930

This document has been produced using
procedures conforming to
BSI 5750 Part 1: 1987; ISO 9001:1987

	Preface	vii
	Synopsis	ix
1.	**Management Summary**	**1**
2.	**Introduction**	**3**
2.1	Purpose	3
2.2	Target Readership	3
2.3	Scope	3
2.4	Context	3
2.5	Related Modules	4
2.5.1	Configuration Management	4
2.5.2	Software Control and Distribution	4
2.5.3	Problem Management	5
2.5.4	Help Desk	5
2.5.5	User Liaison	6
2.5.6	Service Level Management	6
2.5.7	Capacity Management	6
2.5.8	Availability Management	6
2.5.9	Computer Operations Management	7
2.5.10	Network Management	7
2.5.11	Security Management	7
2.5.12	Environmental Infrastructure Modules	7
2.6	Standards	8
3.	**Planning for Change Management**	**9**
3.1	Procedures	9
3.1.1	Planning the Change Management Function	9
3.1.2	Operational Procedures	10
3.1.3	Urgent Changes	21
3.1.4	Interfacing to the Rest of the IT Organization	24
3.1.5	Plan Change Management Reviews	26
3.1.6	Implementation Planning	26
3.2	Dependencies	27
3.2.1	Tools	27
3.2.2	Support Processes	27
3.2.3	Management Commitment	27
3.2.4	Training	27
3.3	People	27
3.3.1	Users and IT Staff	27

3.3.2	Change Manager	27
3.3.3	IT Services Manager	28
3.3.4	CAB Members	28
3.3.5	Contractor's Representatives	29
3.4	Timing	29
3.4.1	Change Advisory Board Meeting	29
3.4.2	Change Schedules	29
3.4.3	Change Slots	30

4.	**Implementation**	**31**
4.1	Procedures	31
4.2	Dependencies	31
4.3	People	31
4.4	Timing	31

5.	**Post-Implementation and Audit**	**33**
5.1	Procedures	33
5.1.1	Review of Change Records	33
5.1.2	Reviewing for Efficiency and Effectiveness	34
5.1.3	Management Reporting	35
5.1.4	Auditing for Compliance	36
5.2	Dependencies	36
5.3	People	37
5.4	Timing	37

6.	**Benefits, Costs and Possible Problems**	**39**
6.1	Benefits	39
6.2	Costs	39
6.2.1	Staff Costs	39
6.2.2	Support tools	40
6.3	Possible Problems	40

7.	**Tools**	**41**

8.	**Conclusions and Recommendations**	**43**

9.	**Further Information**	**45**

Annex A   Glossary of Terms   A-1

Annex B   Job Description - Change Manager   B-1

Annex C   Sample Mission Statement for
          the Change Management Function   C-1

Annex D   Typical Responsibilities - CAB Member   D-1

Annex E   Items to be Included on a Request for Change Form   E-1

Annex F   Example Priority Rating   F-1

Other modules on IT Infrastructure Management in this series.

Preface

Welcome to the IT Infrastructure Library **Change Management** *module.*

In their respective subject areas, the IT Infrastructure Library publications complement and provide more detail than the IS Guides.

The ethos behind the development of the IT Infrastructure Library is the recognition that organizations are becoming increasingly dependent on IT in order to satisfy their corporate aims and meet their business needs. This growing dependency leads to a growing requirement for high-quality IT services. Quality means 'matched to business needs and user requirements as these evolve'.

This module is one of a series of codes of practice intended to facilitate the quality management of IT Services, and of the IT Infrastructure. (By IT Infrastructure, we mean organizations' computers and networks - hardware, software and computer-related telecommunications, upon which applications systems and IT services are built and run). The codes of practice will assist organizations to provide quality IT service in the face of skill shortages, system complexity, rapid change, current and future user requirements, growing user expectations, etc.

Underpinning the IT Infrastructure is the Environmental Infrastructure upon which it is built. Environmental topics are covered in a separate set of guides within the IT Infrastructure Library. Details of these are available from the Information Systems Engineering Group CCTA Rosebery Court.

*IT Infrastructure Management is a complex subject
which for presentational and practical reasons has
been broken down within the IT Infrastructure
Library into a series of modules. A complete list of
current and planned modules is available from the
CCTA Information Systems Engineering Group (see
Section 9).*

*Each IT Infrastructure Management module is
structured in essentially the same way. There is a
Synopsis aimed at Senior Managers (Directors of IT
and above, typically down to Civil Service grade 5); a
Management Summary aimed at Senior IT people and
in some cases 'customers' (typically Civil Service
grades 5 - 7); the main body of the text aimed at IT
middle management (typically grades 7 to HEO); and
technical detail in Annexes.*

*Each module contains **guidance** in Sections 3 to 5;
benefits, costs and possible problems in Section 6,
which may be of interest to senior staff; **tools**
(requirements and examples of real-life availability) in
Section 7; and **conclusions and recommendations**,
also of potential interest to senior staff, in section 8.*

*CCTA is working with the IT trade to foster the
development of software tools to underpin the guidance
contained within the codes of practice (ie to make
adherence to the module more practicable), and
ultimately to automate functions.*

*If you have any comments on this or other modules, do
please let us know. A comment sheet is provided with
every module; please feel free to photocopy it or to let us
have your views via any other medium.*

Thank you. We hope you find this module useful.

Synopsis

Change is a way of life. IT services must change in response to business changes and changing user requirements. Quality of service must be preserved in the face of changes. Quality is necessary because of dependency on IT; without quality, overall costs will be higher, and effectiveness and efficiency of the business lower. This module of the IT Infrastructure Library advises organizations on how to handle IT infrastructure and service changes effectively and efficiently.

1. Management Summary

IT is becoming more integrated into the business of organizations, and more integrated with the work of their staff and customers. As a result, the pace and frequency of change - changing requirements and IT service changes to address the requirements - is increasing. We are also in a period of rapidly changing technology. At the same time business users are expecting and needing high-quality IT services. Therefore organizations need to cope with change without adversely impacting on the quality of IT services.

In fact, experience shows that a high proportion of the IT service quality problems currently being experienced in many organizations can be traced back to a change that has been made to some part of the IT system. The business costs to the organization when such problems do occur are increasingly unacceptable.

A significant improvement in the quality of service offered to users can be achieved if systematic procedures are introduced for the management of change.

This module recommends that organizations establish a single change management function to control and manage changes - proposed and actual - to their operational IT infrastructure. Separate 'project' change management, associated for example with PRINCE, will interface with this function.

The module provides guidance on the processes involved in setting up and maintaining such a change management function.

It describes the important interfaces to other IT infrastructure management functions which are necessary for change management to be fully effective.

In particular it recommends that the logging and control of changes be an integral part of a comprehensive configuration management system.

For change management to be fully effective, adequate support tools are essential. Paper-based systems are difficult to administer except for the smallest IT systems, and are often a cause of inadequate change control and bottlenecks. Section 7 describes the types of tools required and gives examples of those currently available.

The module concludes that all organizations should implement
- if they have not already done so - a comprehensive change
management system to manage the initiation, implementation
and review of all proposed changes to the IT Infrastructure.
Otherwise their IT services - and the business that depends
upon them - are at risk.

2. Introduction

2.1 Purpose

The purpose of this module is to provide guidance to organizations on how to establish a change management function, and the procedures, tools and dependencies that will be necessary to plan for, implement and run change management. The module also describes the benefits that organizations can expect to receive.

2.2 Target Readership

This module of the IT Infrastructure Library is aimed at IT Services Managers and their senior staff, Change Managers and Change Advisory Board (CAB) members. It may also be of interest to Business/User Managers and Applications Development Managers. See section 3.3 for further details.

2.3 Scope

This module recommends, and describes how to implement and run a single centralized change management function for the IT Infrastructure. This function is responsible for managing changes to hardware, communications equipment and software, system software, 'live' applications software and all documentation and procedures that are relevant to the running, support and maintenance of live systems. The function is not responsible for changes to any components - for example, applications software, documentation or procedures - that are under the control of a development project. These will be subject to project change management procedures - for example those associated with PROMPT.

This module does, however, cover the interfaces that will be essential between IT Infrastructure and 'project' change management procedures to ensure that all changes are properly controlled. The guidance provided by the IT Infrastructure Library and for PROMPT are complementary - see Section 3.1.4 for further details.

The module also refers to the need for Configuration Management and Problem Management systems that are integrated with the change management system. It does not, however, cover Configuration and Problem Management systems in detail (separate IT Infrastructure Library modules are available on these).

2.4 Context

This book is one of a series of modules issued as part of the IT Infrastructure Library. Although this module can be read in isolation, it is recommended that it is used in conjunction with the other IT Infrastructure Library modules. Section 2.5 lists the other modules that are most relevant.

2.5 Related Guidance

The following IT Infrastructure Library modules contain advice on topics closely related to change management.

2.5.1 Configuration Management

Change management can be integrated with configuration mangement as a single function: this is the preferred approach. As a minimum it is recommended that the logging and implementation of changes should be done under the control of a comprehensive configuration management system and that the impact assessment of changes is done with the aid of the configuration management system. The configuration management system will identify relationships between an item that is to be changed and any other components of the IT Infrastructure, thus allowing the owners of these components to be involved in the impact assessment process. Whenever a change is made, configuration management records must be updated (see Figure 1). Where possible, this is best accomplished by tools that update records automatically as changes are made.

2.5.2 Software Control and Distribution

Changes will often result in the need for new versions of software to be created, controlled and distributed, as part of a new 'packaged release'. The procedures for achieving this should be closely integrated with those for change management (also shown on Figure 1).

Figure 1:
Relationship with Configuration Management and Software Control & Distribution

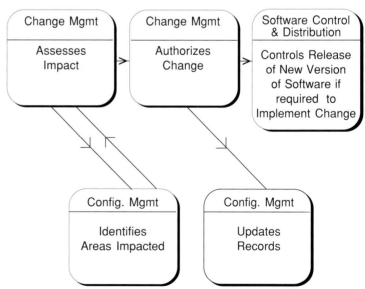

2.5.3 Problem Management

There must be a close interface between the change management and problem management systems. Change requests will often arise as proposed fixes to problems and known errors. If not properly controlled, changes may introduce new problems and errors. For both these reasons a way of tracking back is therefore required. It is recommended that the change and problem records should be held on the same configuration management database, or at least linked without the need for re-keying, to improve the interfaces and ease interrogation and reporting.

An important aspect of problem management is incident control. To recover the IT services from incidents, the three main incident control functions - Help Desk, Computer Operations and Network Management, especially the last two - will normally have delegated authority to implement changes that do not involve a specification change to any configuration item (for example, a fix to a hardware fault). Such changes must however be brought to the subsequent attention of change management and must be recorded in change management records. The problem management and incident control functions will not normally have delegated authority however, to implement changes to correct software errors - other than perhaps reversion to trusted versions. It is recommended that all such changes are assessed for impact via the change management function.

2.5.4 Help Desk

The Help Desk is the single point of contact between IT Services and users, or their representatives, on a day-to-day basis. Optionally, the Help Desk could act as the focal point for change requests from users. The Help Desk will issue Change Schedules and keep users informed of progress on changes. The Change Manager must therefore ensure that the Help Desk is kept constantly aware of change activities.

The Help Desk may be involved alongside User Liaison in assessing changes to decide whether they will be understood and usable. Often changes, particularly if they make the service more complex, will result in more work for the Help Desk.

The Help Desk may be given delegation to implement changes to circumvent incidents within its sphere of authority (see 2.5.9 and 2.5.10 and the Help Desk module). The change management function must be informed about all such changes. Changes that involve a change of specification of any configuration item or a change to an item of software must not, however, be implemented without prior approval by change management.

2.5.5 User Liaison

The User Liaison group will probably act as the focal point for all change requests from users (tool-based change management systems may, however, allow certain users direct submission by electronic means). The User Liaison group should be involved in evaluating changes, to assess whether they will be understood and usable.

User Liaison may need to assist users to articulate their change requests.

2.5.6 Service Level Management

The Service Level Manager is required to adhere to Service Level Agreements (SLAs) and keep any adverse impact on service quality to a minimum. He/she should be involved in assessing the impact of changes upon service quality and SLAs, both when changes are proposed and after they have been implemented. Changes will be proposed at, and be required as follow up action to, Service Quality Reviews and Service Level Agreement reviews.

2.5.7 Capacity Management

Some proposed Requests for Change (RFCs) will arise as a result of capacity management activities (eg tuning, hardware upgrades), and must be subjected to change management procedures. Changes arising from capacity management often require several configuration items, including hardware, software and documentation, to be changed in a carefully synchronized way.

The Capacity Manager must be involved in evaluating all changes, to establish the effect on capacity and performance. This should happen both when changes are proposed and after they are implemented. The Capacity Manager must pay particular attention to the cumulative effect of changes over a period of time. The negligible effect of single changes can often combine to cause degraded response times, file storage problems, and excess demand for processing capacity.

2.5.8 Availability Management

Changes may result from initiatives to improve service reliability and availability. The Availability Manager must be involved in assessing RFCs, to establish the likely effect on reliability and availability, and for reviewing changes implemented for their actual effect on reliability and availability.

2.5.9 Computer Operations Management

The Computer Operations manager must be involved in assessing the impact of proposed changes upon the operations area (eg operational procedures, shift patterns, scheduling) and will also raise RFCs in response to operational problems. The Computer Operations Manager will be responsible for reviewing the effects on operations of actual changes.

The Computer Operations Manager will probably have delegated authority to implement changes (such as hardware repairs) to circumvent incidents within his/her sphere of control. Such changes must be brought to the attention the Change Manager. Changes involving a change to the specification of any configuration item will **not** normally be delegated away from change management.

2.5.10 Network Management

The Network Manager will be responsible for assessing the impact on the network and on network management of proposed changes, and for reviewing the impact of implemented changes. The Network Manager will also be responsible for raising RFCs in connection with the network.

The Network Manager will probably have delegated authority to implement changes to circumvent incidents on the network, providing no specification change to any configuration item is involved. Such delegated changes must be brought to the attention of the change manager, however.

2.5.11 Security Guides

CCTA guidance on IT Security and Privacy is available from the IT Security and Privacy Group at Riverwalk House.

The role of the Security Manager is to assess the impact of proposed changes on security and to raise RFCs in response to security problems. There is also a need to monitor the impact on security of actual changes.

2.5.12 Environmental Infrastructure Modules

Changes to the environment may affect the quality of IT service, and changes to the IT Infrastructure may have implications for the environmental infrastructure. It is recommended that all relevant aspects of the environmental infrastructure are brought under Configuration Management control and subjected to the change management procedures described in this module.

2.6 Standards

The following standards are applicable in the area of change management:

ISO 9000 series, EN29000 and BS5750 - Quality Management and Quality Assurance Standards

The IT Infrastructure Library codes of practice are being designed to assist their users to obtain third-party quality certification. Organizations' internal IT Divisions may wish to be so certified and CCTA may in future recommend that Facilities Management providers are also certified.

PRINCE

PRINCE is the standard Government method for project management. Associated with PRINCE are procedures for controlling changes. This module is intended to complement these procedures by providing guidance on the management of change to the IT infrastructure and services (see Section 3.1.4).

3. Planning for Change Management

This section describes the activities involved in planning for a change management function, and the initial planning activities that will be needed once the function is established.

3.1 Procedures

3.1.1 Planning the Change Management Function

Where there is no existing change management system, the first step must be to appoint, or designate, a Change Manager. An outline Job Description is given in Annex B, and there is additional information in Section 3.3.2. Support staff may be required. Where change management is implemented as part of a wider configuration management function the roles of Change Manager and Configuration Manager may be combined, if scale allows.

The Change Manager's first task will be to agree with the IT Services Manager a mission statement for the change management function, and a way of measuring its efficiency and effectiveness. A suggested mission statement is given at Annex C. The Change Manager's personal objectives and targets should be based on the mission statement and the efficiency and effectiveness of the function.

In devising the mission statement and the success measures, IT Management together with the Change Manager should decide the scope of the change management function. For example, will it be included as part of configuration management or work alongside configuration management (in either case please refer to the configuration management module)? Will it also be responsible for problem management? What scale of changes will it be authorized to approve (see Section 3.1.2.4 for guidance on this)?

The Job Description contained in Annex B should be tailored to take account of these decisions.

In order to ensure that all changes are adequately assessed for impact and resource requirements, a Change Advisory Board (CAB) must be established. The make up of this board must include representatives of all major areas within the IT Services Section, the IT Application Development Section(s) and Senior Users, or their representatives. The Change Manager will act as Chairman of this board. A member of the change management, or configuration management, support staff can act as Secretary. The typical responsibilities of a CAB member are listed at Annex D. As it may not always be possible to convene a full CAB meeting for urgent changes, a CAB Executive Committee (CAB/EC) should also be formed (see section 3.1.3.1 for further details).

Decide whether the change management system is to be a paper-based or a tool-based system. Paper-based systems are inadequate for all except the very smallest of IT systems, and therefore it is strongly recommended that some form of support tool is used, if available. Note, however, that back-up computer or clerical procedures will be required should the primary tool-based system be unavailable owing to hardware failure etc. It is recommended that the logging and implementation of changes is done under the control of an integrated configuration management system, and it is therefore desirable to select a tool which integrates change and configuration management, or can be enhanced or customized to do so. Information on support tools is given in Section 7.

Procurement of support tools, setting up of the data (ie configuration inventory data, change authorities etc), and staff training and familiarization with the support tools must be completed prior to implementation.

3.1.2 Operational Procedures
When appointed, the Change Manager must plan the implementation of operational procedures as described in the following paragraphs, or amend any existing procedures to conform to these guidelines. Figure 2 gives a flow chart of these procedures.

.1 Requests For Change (RFC)
Requests for Change will be triggered for a wide variety of reasons, from a wide variety of sources. These reasons will include:

* as a resolution to an Incident or Problem Report

* in response to user dissatisfaction expressed via User Liaison or the Service Level Manager

* because of the proposed introduction of a new configuration item (CI)

* because of a proposed upgrade to some component of the IT infrastructure

* as a result of changed business requirements or direction

* as a result of new or changed legislation

* in response to product or service changes from vendors or contractors.

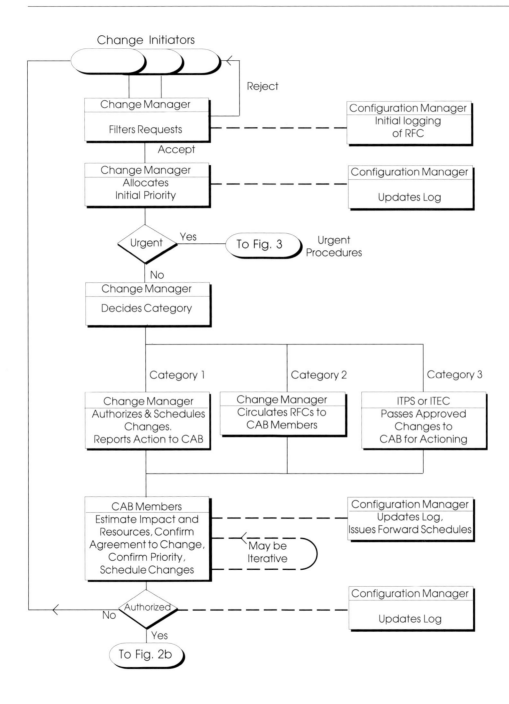

Figure 2a: Normal Change Control Procedures

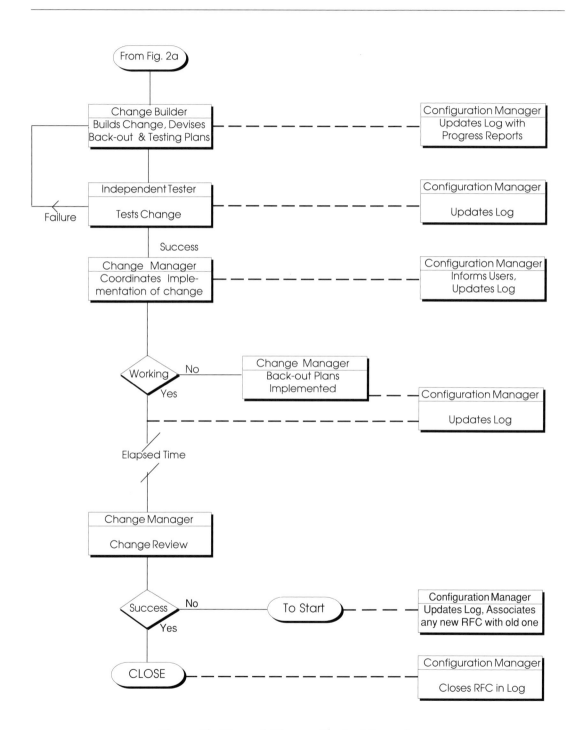

Figure 2b: Normal Change Control Procedures

(3.1.2 continued)

RFCs can be concerned with any part of the IT infrastructure or with any service or activity associated with it. Here are some examples:

* hardware

* software

* telecommunications facilities

* engineering cover

* training courses

* IT infrastructure management procedures

* tactical plans

* environmental infrastructure.

Certain changes that do not affect the specification of configuration items - for example a hardware repair - may not need to be impact assessed in advance. However it is recommended that changes to correct software errors are subject to formal RFCs and impact assessment.

Procedures for documenting RFCs, using standard forms or screens, must be decided. Where a computer-based support tool is used, the format may be decided by the tool. Where no standard is imposed by a support tool, or if a paper based system has to be used, it is recommended that the items shown in Annex E are included on the Request for Change form.

It is recommended that all members of the IT Division be authorized to request changes, otherwise innovation might be stifled, or important concerns may go unreported. Where there are large numbers of users, it is suggested that user requests should require signature by a senior User Manager prior to submission. This will filter out any requests that do not have the support of the wider user community, or are impractical, and help collate similar or identical requests, thus reducing volumes. However, User Managers must also be careful not to stifle innovation and not to discourage staff from proposing changes.

.2 Change Logging

All RFCs received must be logged and allocated an identification number (in chronological sequence). **Where change requests are submitted as a resolution to a Problem Report (PR) it is important that the original PR number is retained** so that the link between the problem and resolution is readily apparent.

(3.1.2 continued)

It is recommended that the logging of RFCs is done by means of a comprehensive configuration management system, capable of storing data on all configuration items and also, importantly, the relationships between them. This will greatly assist when assessing the likely impact of a change to one component of the system on all other components.

Change management may be made an integral part of this configuration management system.

Procedures need to specify who will have access to the logging system, and what the levels of access will be. Normally it will be open to any authorized personnel to create, or add reports of progress to an RFC (though the support tool must keep the Change Manager aware of such actions), but only the Change Manager or his staff, or configuration management support staff if change management is an integral part of a configuration management system, will be able to delete an RFC.

The procedures should stipulate that as changes are logged, the Change Manager should briefly consider each request and filter out any that are totally impractical. These should be returned to the initiator, together with brief details of the reason for the rejection, and the log should record this fact. A right of appeal against rejection must exist, via normal management channels, and must be incorporated within the procedures.

.3 Allocation of Priorities

Every RFC must be allocated a priority which indicates the urgency with which the change should be considered by the CAB(if appropriate) and effected. The Change Manager should be made responsible for assigning this priority. The priority of RFCs must be decided in collaboration with the initiator, but it should not be left to the initiator alone, as a higher priority than is really justified may result.

The purpose of many RFCs will be to address Problems and correct Known Errors. Such items will have already have been issued a severity code which indicates the urgency with which they should be 'fixed'. This severity code should be reviewed and (unless there is a good reason why not) should be used as a basis for the change priority.

A suggested priority system is shown at Annex F. Separate procedures are required for Priority 0 (Urgent) changes. These procedures are described in section 3.1.3. The rest of this section deals with non-urgent RFCs.

.4 Change Categorization

The Change Manager must examine each non-urgent RFC, and decide how to proceed based on which of three pre-defined categories the RFC falls into. These categories are:

1   Minor impact only, and few 'build' or additional 'run-time' resources required. The Change Manager should have delegated authority to authorize and schedule such changes; these must be reported, however, to the CAB and to IT Services management. If the Change Manager has any doubts about authorizing any such change he/she can optionally refer it to the CAB for a wider assessment.

2   More than minor impact and/or significant build or run-time resources required. The RFC must be tabled for discussion at the next Change Advisory Board (CAB) meeting. Prior to the meeting all documentation should be circulated to the CAB, and possibly a wider audience (eg hardware engineers) if deemed necessary by the Change Manager or CAB members, for impact and resource assessment. See 3.1.2.6.

3   Major impact, and/or very large amount of build or run-time resources required, or impact upon other parts of the IT organization (see Section 3.1.4). The RFC must be referred to the Director of IT, for discussion and a policy decision by the IT Planning Secretariat (ITPS), or the IT Executive Committee (ITEC). Such changes, once approved by the ITPS or ITEC, must be passed back down via the CAB for scheduling and implementation.

It is envisaged that the vast majority of RFCs will fall into categories 1 and 2.

.5 CAB Meetings

CAB meetings should have a standard agenda which should include:

1   changes applied without reference to the CAB by:

-   incident control - problem management

-   change management

2   RFCs to be assessed by CAB members

3   RFCs that have been assessed by CAB members

4   change reviews.

Papers should be circulated in advance to allow CAB members (and others who are required by the Change Manager or CAB members) to do impact and resource assessment (Agenda item 2 - see next section).

(3.1.2 continued)

In some circumstances it will be desirable to table RFCs at one CAB meeting to enable the Change Manager briefly to explain them before CAB members take the papers away for consideration in time for the next meeting (Agenda item 3).

Change reviews are covered in section 3.1.2.12 (page 20).

.6 Impact and Resource Assessment

When conducting the impact and resource assessment for RFCs referred to them, the CAB, and any others (nominated by the Change Manager or CAB Members) who are involved in this process, must consider the following items:

* the effect upon the IT infrastructure and the user service

    - capacity and performance

    - reliability and resilience

    - contingency plans

    - security

* the impact on other services which run on the same IT Infrastructure (or on software development projects)

* the effect of **not** implementing the change

* the resources required to implement the change, covering the likely costs, the number and availability of people required, the elapsed time, any new IT Infrastructure required

* additional ongoing resource required if the change is implemented.

Based upon these impact and resource assessments, and the potential benefits of the change, each assessor must indicate whether he/she supports approval of the change, in principle. CAB members should in addition decide whether they are content with the priority ratings allocated by the Change Manager and be prepared to argue for any alterations they see as necessary.

.7 CAB Recommendations

CAB members must come to the meetings prepared to make a decision on which changes should go ahead on the priority of these changes, and on their scheduling (next section). The CAB should be informed of any changes that have been implemented as circumventions to incidents and should be given the opportunity to recommend follow-up action to these.

Note that the CAB is an advisory body only. The final decision on whether to authorize changes, and commit to the expense involved, remains the responsibility of IT Management (normally the Director of IT or the IT Services Manager, or the Change Manager as their delegated representative). The change management procedures must specifically name the person(s) authorized to sign off RFCs.

.8 Change Scheduling

Wherever possible, the CAB must schedule approved changes into target 'releases' and recommend allocation of resources accordingly. In doing this, the CAB must take account of the resource requirements of minor changes scheduled by the Change Manager. **Note: a 'release' is a collection of new and changed configuration items which are tested and introduced into the live environment together.**

As a general principle it is advisable to make no more than one change at a time, as this aids diagnosis should errors result. However, this is usually impractical. For example, a hardware change may require an operating system change to support it; applications software may need to be changed so rapidly that a policy of 'one change at a time' is impracticably slow; a simple software change may require simultaneous introduction of new documentation, procedures and training. Multiple changes should be packaged into a 'release' so that the whole release can be backed out if problems occur.

Software changes are normally implemented in the form of package releases, which may incorporate a number of separate changes to resolve a number of known errors, or implement new features. It is very important to have a clearly defined software product release strategy which interfaces to the change management system. For further information on this please see the **Software Control and Distribution** Module.

Part of the change scheduling exercise will involve ensuring that the estimated resources and costs of the change are within the overall budget (staff resources and money) available for the target release. If they are not, this will delay the release and/or cause it to go over budget. If a delay or extra costs are unacceptable, re-scheduling will be necessary. It should be noted that, generally speaking, the later you wait to schedule, or re-schedule, a change within the release building phase, the more it will cost. This is due to the extra effort involved in reworking the contents of the release. Work on some changes may have to be delayed or scrapped in order to accommodate other changes that are scheduled late. It is therefore essential to plan ahead, and implement changes as far as possible in accordance with 'normal' release planning parameters.

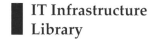
(3.1.2 continued)

It is important to limit the size of releases to manageable proportions. It is unlikely that any release will be completely fault free. It therefore follows that the larger the release, the more effort will be required to identify and address any new errors. There will be a growth in support activities, such as Help Desk calls, following a new release. It is important that staff are not swamped with work they cannot deal with, as this will have an adverse impact on service quality. Over a period of time experience will give an indication of what can be handled, and these limits should be adhered to.

In reviewing outstanding RFCs, the CAB should take account of package release schedules and decide whether to recommend increasing the priorities and/or allocating additional resources to allow particular changes associated with the RFCs to be incorporated in scheduled releases. In doing this the CAB will have to review previously agreed schedules, and make any amendments that are necessary.

It is recommended that forward change schedules are issued following each CAB meeting. These should include details of all changes that have been authorized for implementation in the next 3 months, and the release(s) that they have been allocated to. Brief details of changes planned for the next 2 years should also be included. It is obvious that only major changes, such as machine upgrades, can be predicted so far in advance. For convenience it may be advantageous to issue the short and long term schedules separately, as the short term schedule will be more volatile, and the longer term schedule will be aimed at higher-level staff.

Change schedules must be distributed to all users or their representatives, application developers, IT Services staff including the Help Desk, and any other interested parties. Distribution of change schedules outside IT Services should be done via the Help Desk or User Liaison functions.

.9 Change Building

Authorized RFCs must be passed to the relevant technical groups for 'building' of the changes. This might involve creating a new version of one or more software modules, preparing a hardware modification, producing new or amended documentation, preparing amendments to user training etc, or a combination of such tasks. The Change Manager has a coordination role, supported by normal line management controls, to ensure that these activities are resourced, and completed to schedule.

It is important to ensure that the same standards and methods - such as SSADM - that were used to achieve the highest possible quality for the original component are again used for the change. Where a change is made which affects previously baselined documents, such as original design specifications, these should be brought up to date.

Back-out procedures must be prepared and documented in advance, for each authorized change, so that if problems occur after implementation these procedures can be quickly activated with minimum impact on service quality. Back-out generally means reversion to a previous, trusted version or state. The Change Manager must not allow any change to progress unless these back-out procedures are provided.

.10 Change Testing

To prevent changes adversely impacting on IT service quality it is strongly recommended that changes should be thoroughly tested in advance (including back-out procedures where possible). Testing should cover performance, security, maintainability, supportability and reliability/availability as well as functionality. In many cases this will require a separate 'test environment'. Where no such environment exists, plans should be made to create one. To avoid collusion (for example, to protect vested interests) or errors, it is recommended that this testing should be carried out independently from the change builders and the results subjected to QA audit. Separate modules covering Testing and Quality Assurance are available which address these subjects in more detail.

It is recognized that it will not be possible fully to test all changes in advance. It may be possible in some instances to use modelling techniques to assess the likely impact of a change, instead of, or in addition to, testing. This approach is particularly useful in the area of capacity/performance. Once a model is set up, the Capacity Manager can for example easily assess the likely impact on response times of a critical file being moved from one disc to another.

In all cases involving changes that have not been fully tested, special care needs to be taken over implementation (see below).

The Change Manager has an overseeing role to ensure that all changes that can be, are thoroughly tested.

.11 Change Implementation

The Change Manager has responsibility for ensuring that changes are implemented as scheduled, though this will be largely a coordination role as the actual implementation will be the responsibility of others (eg engineers will implement hardware changes).

(3.1.2 continued)

Procedures are required to ensure that all relevant staff, particularly users, are advised prior to the implementation of changes, via the Help Desk.

Special care is required where changes that have only been partially tested are to be implemented. The implementation of such changes must be scheduled when the least impact on live services is likely, and support staff must be on hand to deal quickly with any problems that might arise. Where it is possible to introduce such changes into a limited environment, eg for a pilot group of users, this should be considered.

.12 Change Review

All implemented changes must be reviewed by the Change Manager after a pre-defined period has elapsed. He/she should involve CAB members and look to them for assistance in the review process. Change reviews should be tabled at CAB meetings, for CAB members' information and to agree any follow-up action that may be needed. The purpose of these reviews is to establish that:

* the change has had the desired effect and met its objectives

* users are content with the results.

* there have been no unexpected or undesirable side-effects (eg functionality, capacity/performance, security, maintainability)

* the resources used to implement the change were as planned.

Any problems and discrepancies must be fed back to CAB members, impact assessors, product authorities and 'release' authorities, to improve the estimating processes for the future.

Where a change has not achieved its objectives the CAB must decide what follow up action is required. This could even involve raising a revised RFC.

If the review is satisfactory or the original change is abandoned, the RFC must be formally closed in the logging system.

Procedures for automatically prompting reviews of implemented changes must be devised. The review period should be separately defined for each change, and will depend on the nature of the change (eg changes to a software application that is run several times a day can be reviewed after a week or two, but changes to a monthly run suite could only be reviewed after several months have elapsed). Incidents and problems arising from a change will of course be fed back immediately into the problem management system, and could then trigger further RFCs. These incidents, problems and RFCs must be traceable back to the original 'offending' change. The content and timing of the review of that change will be consequentially affected.

The Change Manager must regularly review, and present to the CAB, all outstanding changes awaiting implementation. If necessary, the priority levels of these changes should be adjusted by the CAB to take account of changed circumstances, age of the request etc.

3.1.3 Urgent Changes

The number of priority 0 (urgent) proposed changes must be kept to an absolute minimum. All changes likely to be required should be foreseen, planned for, and submitted to the CAB in good time, bearing in mind the availability of resources to build and test the changes.

Incident control staff within the Computer Operations and Network Management functions (and possibly Help Desk staff) may have delegated authority to circumvent certain types of incident (eg hardware failure) without prior authorization by change management. Such circumventions should be limited to actions that do not change the specification of configuration items and that do not attempt to correct software errors.

The preferred route for circumventing incidents caused by software errors must be to revert to the previous trusted state, or version, rather than attempting an unplanned and potentially dangerous change. Even for such a reversion, organizations may decide in general to require change authorization, but to give Operations or Problem Management support staff delegated authority to carry out limited pre-defined reversions in some circumstances, such as overnight periods, when the Change Manager is not present.

Nevertheless occasions will occur when urgent changes are essential and so procedures must be devised to deal with them quickly, without sacrificing normal management controls. Procedures must therefore be devised as shown in Figure 3, and described in the following paragraphs.

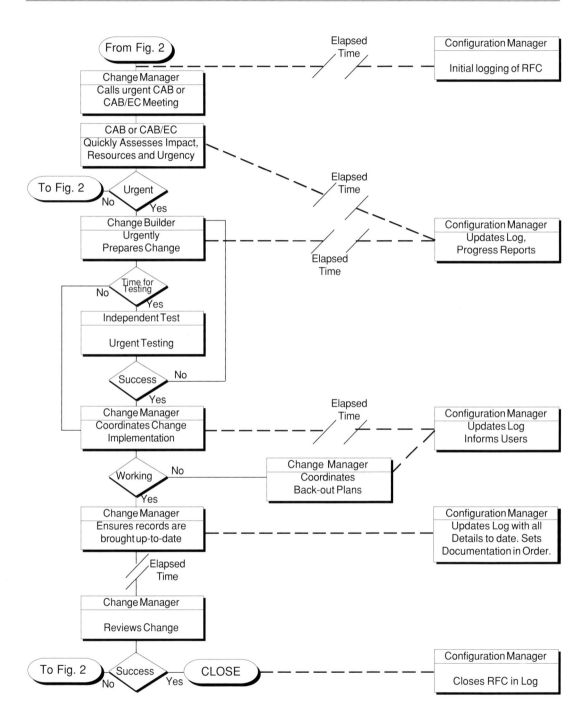

Figure 3: Urgent Change Procedures

3.1.3.1 Impact and Resource Assessment of Urgent Changes

Ideally all changes must be fully assessed for impact and resource requirements. If time permits, the Change Manager must convene an urgent meeting of the CAB to carry out this function. Should there be insufficient time available to summon the full CAB, then the assessment will have to be limited to Change Advisory Board Executive Committee (CAB/EC) members who, if necessary, must be contacted by paging device or telephone at home. The CAB/EC must include staff capable of understanding both the business and the technical implications of a proposed change, and able to estimate resource requirements. It is recommended that the CAB/EC should consist of the Change Manager, plus two or three others. Normally these will be a Senior User Manager, the Problem Manager and the Service Level Manager, but some flexibility should be allowed (eg if a database corruption occurs, involve the Database Administrator; if security is threatened, involve the Security Manager).

The CAB (or CAB/EC) must decide whether the change warrants urgent action and, if so, will recommend implementation of the change. If the CAB decides that urgent action is not required the proposed change should be tabled for the next scheduled CAB meeting.

All actions should be recorded, as they are carried out, within the change management log. If this is not possible for any reason then they must be manually recorded for inclusion at the next possible opportunity.

.2 Urgent Change Building

Approved changes must be allocated to the relevant technical group for building. Where timescales demand it, the Change Manager must, in collaboration with the appropriate technical manager, ensure that sufficient staff and IT resources (machine time etc) are available to do this work, even if this means calling staff in from home. Procedures and agreements - approved and supported by IT Management - must be in place which allow for this. Back-out plans must still be devised despite the urgency of the change.

The Change Manager must give as much advance warning as possible to the users about the imminent change. This should be done via the Help Desk, if it is available.

.3 Testing of Urgent Changes

As much testing of the change as is possible should be carried out. Completely untested changes should not be implemented if at all avoidable. Experience has shown that when changes go wrong the cost is usually greater than that of adequate testing.

.4 Implementation of Urgent Changes

When urgent changes are implemented, particularly those that have not been adequately tested, the Change Manager must ensure that an adequate technical presence is available, to tackle any incidents or problems that may occur. The IT systems and service(s) should not be taken down to implement an urgent change unless it is absolutely necessary, particularly if this means violating SLAs.

If the change, once implemented, fails to rectify the urgent outstanding problem, there may need to be iterative attempts at fixes. It is important that each iteration is controlled in the manner described in this section. The Change Manager should ensure abortive changes are swiftly backed out. If too many attempts at an urgent change are abortive, this suggests a need for better testing. In such circumstances, it may be better to provide a partial service, with some user facilities withdrawn, to allow the change to be thoroughly tested, then to suspend the whole service and try to implement the change in great haste.

.5 Record Completion

It may not be possible to update all change management records at the time that urgent actions are being completed (eg during overnight or weekend working). It is however essential that manual records are made during such periods, and it will be the responsibility of the Change Manager to ensure that all records are completed retrospectively, at the earliest possible opportunity. This is vital to ensure valuable management information is not lost.

.6 Reviews of Urgent Changes

Once successfully implemented, urgent changes should be treated in the same way as all other changes and the change reviews described earlier in Section 3.1.2.12 must be carried out.

3.1.4 Interfacing to the Rest of the IT Organization

This module describes how to manage changes to components of the 'live' IT Infrastructure and services, or to services that are being provided in support of applications software development. **It does not cover changes to items under the control of other parts of the IT organization (eg changes to be managed as part of a software development project controlled under PRINCE).**

However, there will be occasions when a proposed change to the IT infrastructure potentially has a wider impact upon other parts of the organization (eg impact upon applications development projects; impact upon the business organization), or vice versa.

Where a wider impact is perceived the RFC must be referred via the Director of IT to the IT Planning Secretariat(ITPS). The ITPS deal with day-to-day activities on behalf of the IT Executive Committee (ITEC), and will be responsible for coordinating an impact and resource assessment of the RFC across all relevant parts of the organization, and will then decide if the change is to be approved. Where necessary, the ITPS will submit RFCs to the ITEC for approval.

Any actions arising from an RFC approved by other parts of the IT organization, or as a result of changes proposed from other parts of the organization which impact upon the IT Infrastructure (eg business or legislative changes) will be passed back down to the CAB for scheduling and implementation.

Plans must be made to ensure the IT infrastructure and other change management systems are effectively interfaced to each other. The change management authorities in other parts of the IT organization must be involved in setting up these interfaces, and IT management commitment will be needed to ensure they work.

The assessment of whether a proposed change to the IT Infrastructure and services will impact upon other parts of the IT organization and vice-versa will be much easier to establish, and far less subjective, if a single configuration management system is used to control all IT configuration items (CIs). Such a system will identify the relationships between the CI proposed for change and other CIs that may be affected. The owners of such CIs can then be contacted as part of the assessment process. Figure 4 (overleaf) illustrates the use of a single configuration management system to identify the impact of IT infrastructure changes on PRINCE projects. Please refer to the **Configuration Management** module for guidance on setting up a configuration management system.

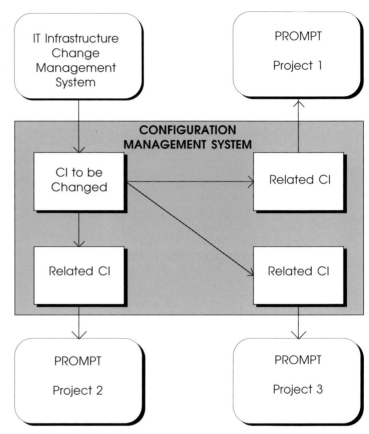

**Figure 4:
Interfaces to PROMPT
Project Change
Management Systems**

3.1.5 Plan Change Management Reviews

Plans should be made for the change management reviews, metrics, management reports and audits described in detail in section 5.

3.1.6 Implementation Planning

Plans should be made to bring the change management system into service. These plans should include installation and test plans for any software tools and training plans for change management staff, other IT staff and users. Publicity material and any seminars should be prepared in readiness for a change management launch. Emphasis should be placed on selling the benefits to both IT staff and users (see section 6 for further information on this).

3.2 Dependencies

3.2.1 Tools

Paper-based change management systems are inadequate for most IT systems, and so support tools will normally be required. Section 7 describes the requirements for change management tools and gives some information on tools currently available.

3.2.2 Support Processes

For change management to be fully effective a number of supporting processes will be required. These include Problem Management, Configuration Management, Help Desk and Software Control & Distribution, as described in the IT Infrastructure Library modules on these subjects.

3.2.3 Management Commitment

Management commitment will be required to ensure that adequate resources are made available, and also to ensure that an adequate level of discipline is engendered amongst all IT Services staff to prevent circumvention of change management procedures. Ask the Director of IT to speak at introductory seminars to announce the new procedures and/or sign any publicity material used.

3.2.4 Training

Staff training will be required in the new change management procedures and in the use of support tools.

3.3 People

3.3.1 Users and IT Staff

Users and IT staff must be aware of the change management procedures. Make it clear that these are mandatory and ensure that it is not possible for changes to be implemented outside of the change management system.

3.3.2 Change Manager

A job description for this role is given at Annex B. The Change Manager is directly responsible to the IT Services manager and will be a peer to other managers within the IT Services Section (see 3.3.3). It will be prudent to nominate a deputy Change Manager to cover absences etc.

In large organizations this will be a full-time post, and may require support staff (particularly if change management is not supported by configuration management and software tools). In small organizations this post should have responsibility for other IT Infrastructure Management tasks, such as configuration management and problem management.

3.3.3 IT Services Manager

The IT Services Manager is the head of the IT Service Section, and has overall responsibility for service quality. Typically the IT Services Manager is a peer to the Applications Development Manager(s) and the Administration and Finance Manager, and they are all responsible to the Director of IT (see Figure 5).

The Change Manager is directly responsible to, and will require the support of, the IT Services Manager to ensure that the correct level of importance is given to change management procedures.

Figure 5:
Management Structure

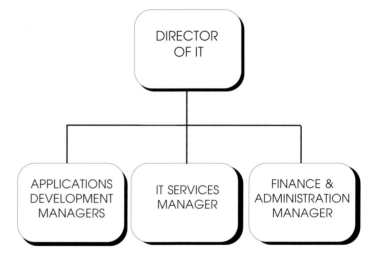

3.3.4 CAB Members

The CAB must be capable of ensuring that all changes are adequately assessed from both a business and a technical viewpoint.

It is suggested that CAB membership should consist of:

*   The Change Manager

*   User Managers

*   User Group Representatives

*   Applications Developers/Maintainers (as appropriate)

*   Software Control & Distribution Manager

*   Other IT Services Staff as required

*   Office Services staff (where IT changes may affect accommodation and vice versa)

*   Contractors' representatives as required (see 3.3.5).

The change procedures must specifically name the CAB members, and CAB/EC members.

CAB meetings could represent a potentially large overhead on the time of CAB Members. Therefore all RFCs must be circulated in advance, and flexibility allowed to CAB members on whether to attend in person, to send a deputy, or to send any comments via the Change Manager.

3.3.5 Contractors' Representatives

It is essential to ensure that contractors' representatives (eg hardware engineers, environmental or accommodation maintenance staff) are aware of, and adhere to, the organization's change management procedures. For example the organization will wish to prevent unauthorized changes to hardware and microcode by hardware engineers; and unauthorized changes to software by suppliers' staff via on-line support facilities. Remember that even environmental or accommodation changes can impact upon IT services, so contractors dealing with accommodation and environment should also be subjected to change management procedures.

3.4 Timing

It is recommended that any installation that does not already have a formal change management system should start planning for one immediately, with a view to implementing it as soon as possible.

It is likely to be 1-3 months from the start of the planning stage before the new system is ready for implementation, though this time could be extended if a support tool is to be procured and set-up, particularly if a tool which integrates change and configuration management is to be used. Lead times must be established and taken into account.

3.4.1 Change Advisory Board Meetings

The frequency and duration of CAB meetings will depend upon the scale and volatility of the installation. If short but frequent meetings are held this is likely to cause less of a change-bottleneck than longer, but less frequent meetings. It is recommended that the interval between CAB meetings should not exceed 20 working days (although during periods of high volatility some installations may require meetings 2 to 3 times a week), and that the duration of meetings should not exceed 2 hours.

3.4.2 Change Schedules

Forward change schedules must be issued following each CAB meeting. These should include all details of changes to be implemented in the next 3 months, and brief details of changes planned for the next 2 years. For convenience these may be held as two separate documents. Note that most changes will be scheduled for a particular release package. It is not always possible to predict the actual dates when releases will be ready.

3.4.3 Change Slots

The timing of changes can be very important. Serious consideration should be given to the introduction of regular 'change slots' - times when changes can be implemented with minimal impact upon user service (eg between 1800hrs and 2000hrs Tuesdays and Thursdays). Such slots should, of course, be agreed with the Users. If testing of changes has to be carried out in a non-dedicated environment consideration might also be given to 'test slots'.

4. Implementation

4.1 Procedures

When all the planning processes are completed and change management is ready for implementation, the Change Manager must ensure that all the affected parties are informed in advance about the implementation date, and the new procedures to be followed. For staff outside IT Services, this should be done via the Help Desk.

It is unlikely to be practical to parallel-run change management systems, so when implementing an IT Infrastructure Library change management system a direct cut-over from any previous system is recommended.

Any changes that were initiated via an old change management system, or without being subjected to change management, must be transferred into the new system at implementation time.

Any initial difficulties with the new change management system should be identified as quickly as possible after implementation and resolved (see section 5.1.3). It should not be necessary to 'back out' the new system. Any support tools should be thoroughly tested before 'go live'. If there are any problems with support tools, it may be necessary to temporarily revert to manual methods. These are, however, likely to be slow and inefficient.

4.2 Dependencies

As section 3.2.

4.3 People

The Change Manager will be responsible for overseeing implementation of the new change management system. The Help Desk will liaise with all users to keep them informed.

IT Management support will be needed to resource the CAB and give it the appropriate level of authority, to promote the change management system, and to overcome any resistance to formalized change management.

4.4 Timing

Implementation must not begin until the manual/tool-based system is ready, until the CAB is set-up, and until everyone is aware of and trained in the new procedures.

The Change Manager, in collaboration with the Service Level Manager, must liaise with other IT Managers and User Managers to set an implementation date and time which will have the least potential adverse effect on IT service quality (eg during periods of low work throughput).

Implementation of the new change management system will
be easier if, where possible, it can be timed to allow change
activity to be kept to an absolute minimum, immediately prior
to and during the implementation. This may not be possible,
however, if the new system is being introduced to counter
problems arising from inadequate change management.

5. Post-implementation and Audit

5.1 Procedures

The day-to-day operational procedures to be followed for progressing individual RFCs should already have been planned, as described in Section 3. Additionally, the following procedures must be carried out.

5.1.1 Review of Change Records

The Change Manager must periodically review change records - with whatever support is available from software tools - to identify any trends that occur. Specific things to look for include:

* amount of RFCs

* proportion of RFCs rejected

* number of implemented changes (broken down by configuration item)

* number of changes backed out

* proportion of implemented changes that are not successful (in total and broken down by configuration item)

* change backlogs, broken down by configuration item and by stage in the change management process.

All of these items should be broken down by change priority. Priority 0 'urgent' changes should be included.

This information can be used as a basis for assessing the efficiency and effectiveness of the change management function (see 5.1.2), and for management reporting (see 5.1.3). For the former, it is necessary to 'disentangle' effects that are outside the direct control of change management. For example, frequent changes affecting a particular configuration item may be a result of fragility of that item, and not a bad reflection on change management as might at first sight be thought. Frequent changes in user facilities might reflect a rapidly-changing user requirement.

The Change Manager should instigate follow-up actions to correct any problems or inefficiencies in the change management system. For example, a large change backlog may indicate that change management is under-resourced; a high incidence of unsuccessful changes indicates that change assessment or change building is not working satisfactorily.

Change record reviews may also show up problems in other
functions such as problem management; in the reliability of
system components; or in staff's or users' procedures and/or
training. These problems should be reported to the managers
concerned and highlighted in the change management reports
to IT management (see 5.1.3).

**5.1.2. Reviewing for
Efficiency and Effectiveness**

It is recommended that the change management function be
periodically reviewed by IT Services management for efficiency
and effectiveness.

Such a review should be carried out shortly after the change
management system is implemented, to ensure that the plans
were carried out correctly and that the system is functioning as
intended. Any problems should be traced back to source and
corrected as soon as possible after implementation of the
change management system. Thereafter regular formal reviews
should take place - at least every 6 months (the Change
Manager should, however, **continually** assess the efficiency
and effectiveness of the change management system).

A high number of changes does not necessarily indicate any
problem with the change management system - it may just
reflect a volatile IT system and any attempt to reduce the
number of RFCs may stifle innovation. However an efficient
and effective change management function must show a clear
indication of the following:

* a reduction of adverse impact on IT service quality
  resulting from poor change management

* a reduction in the number of PRs traced back to changes
  implemented

* a reduction in the number of changes backed-out

* a reduction in the number of urgent (and therefore
  unplanned) changes

* no evidence of changes having been made without reference
  to the change management system

* close correlation between forward schedules and actual
  implementation of changes

* no high priority RFCs in backlogs, and the size of backlogs
  not increasing

* evidence of accurate resource estimating, when resource estimates are retrospectively compared with actual resources used

* regular reviewing of RFCs and implemented changes, and clearing of review backlogs

* successful implementation of changes that give a positive benefit to the running of the organization's business, or the satisfaction of the users

* a low incidence of unjustifiably rejected RFCs.

These items can be used as metrics for measuring the effectiveness and, to an extent, the efficiency of the change management function.

In measuring the efficiency of the change management function it will be necessary to consider the assessors, builders, testers, etc, and the amount of change successfully implemented per unit of staff costs. This may not be easy to interpret in absolute terms, but it should generally be possible to observe an increase in efficiency over time - most noticeably in the early days of the change management function.

5.1.3 Management Reporting   Regular summaries of changes must be provided to IT and User management. Different management levels are likely to require different levels of information, ranging from the IT Services Manager who may require a detailed weekly report, to the senior IT management committees which are likely only to require a quarterly management summary.

Consider including the following statistics:

* number of changes implemented in the period, in total and by configuration item

* a breakdown of the reasons for change (user requests for enhancements, business requirements, incident/problem fixes, procedures/training improvement,etc)

* number of changes successful

* number of changes backed-out and reasons (eg incorrect assessment, bad build)

* number of problems traced to changes (broken down into problem severity levels) and reasons (eg incorrect assessment, bad build)

* number of RFCs and implemented changes reviewed, and size of review backlogs broken down over time

* draw special attention to high incidences of RFCs/PRs relating to one Configuration Item and give the reasons (eg volatile user requirement, fragile component, bad build)

* figures from previous periods (last period, last year) for comparison.

5.1.4 Auditing for Compliance

This sub-section is a checklist for organizations that wish to audit their change management function (using the organizations' computer audit section, which is independent of the IT Services section), for compliance to the procedures and advice in this module. It is recommended that such an audit is completed at least annually, and it may be required more often, initially or where particular problems are evident.

The following items should be examined:

* randomly selected RFCs

* change records

* CAB minutes

* change schedules

* review records for random RFCs and implemented changes.

Checks must be made to ensure that:

* all RFCs have been correctly logged, assessed and actioned

* change schedules have been adhered to, or there is a good reason why not

* all items raised at CAB meetings have been followed up and resolved

* all change reviews have been carried out on time

* all documentation is accurate, up-to-date and complete.

5.2 Dependencies

In addition to the dependencies shown in Section 3.2, the following will be required:

* report production facilities, in order to produce management reports - these facilities may be provided by the change management software tools

* audit trails, to simplify the process of auditing for compliance - these will need to be built in to the change management tools and procedures.

5.3 People

The Change Manager has primary responsibility for ensuring that change management procedures are properly adhered to, though the Change Manager must be supported in this role by all managers in the IT Division, and also User Managers.

The Director of IT should arrange for regular efficiency and effectiveness reviews of the change management function to be carried out under the direction of the IT Services Manager.

It is recommended that an independent audit, by the organization's Computer Audit section, is carried out regularly (at least annually) to ensure compliance with change management procedures.

5.4 Timing

The frequency and duration of CAB meetings should be as described in Section 3.4.

The frequency with which the Change Manager is able to review change records (5.1.1) will depend upon the type of logging system used. An integrated support tool should provide data in the required format quickly enough to allow this to be done on an almost day-to-day basis. Paper-based systems will require some manual analysis and reporting, and so will probably not allow reviews to take place more frequently than weekly, perhaps even monthly if a lot of changes occur and there are few support staff.

The IT Services Manager should review the efficiency and effectiveness of the change management function regularly, at least every six months (see 5.1.2). A review should take place shortly after the change management system has been brought into use (say 1 to 3 months after) and the regular reviews should take place say every 2 to 4 months for the first few times until confidence is established that the system is functioning satisfactorily. The Change Manager should keep the effectiveness and efficiency of change management under **continual** review.

Arrange an independent audit of the change management function for compliance to the procedures and guidance contained in this module, at least annually.

The suggested frequency of management reporting (5.1.3) is as follows:

*   to the IT Services Manager - weekly or more frequently, depending on the quality and stability of services

*   to the Director of IT and senior User Managers - monthly

*   to the senior IT committees - quarterly.

6. Benefits, Costs and Possible Problems

6.1 Benefits

Effective change management is indispensable to the satisfactory provision of IT services. An ability to absorb a high level of change is necessary for **effective** IT Service Provision. An ability to change things in an orderly way, without making errors and taking wrong decisions is necessary for **efficient** IT Service Provision.

Specific benefits from an effective change management system include:

* less adverse impact of changes on the quality of IT services, and Service Level Agreements

* a better assessment of the cost of proposed changes, before they are incurred

* a reduction in the number of changes that have to be 'backed-out', but an ability to do this more easily when necessary

* the accumulation of valuable management information relating to changes, which will help diagnose problem areas and assist the Problem Manager, Availability Manager etc

* increased productivity of users - due to less disrupted, higher quality IT services

* increased productivity of key IT personnel - no longer having to be diverted from planned duties to implement urgent changes, or back-out erroneous changes

* an ability to absorb a high level of change (which is becoming the norm) without difficulty.

6.2 Costs

6.2.1 Staff Costs

There will be staff costs for the Change Manager, the change management team, CAB members and change builders but these must be balanced against the benefits that will be gained. In practice in most organizations there will already be a number of people who are spending time on handling changes.

Although adherence to the guidance in this module may appear to increase the amount of management time spent in dealing with changes, in practice management will spend less time handling problems arising from ineffective change management.

6.2.2 Support Tools

The cost of support tools, together with any hardware requirements, needs to be considered. Although tools that integrate support for change management, configuration management, problem management and help desks are likely to be more expensive than 'simple' change management tools, the additional cost will often be justified. For larger systems these management processes will be virtually impossible without adequate support tools.

6.3 Possible Problems

Paper-based systems are difficult to administer and often result in bottlenecks.

There may be cultural difficulties in getting IT staff and users to accept that a single change management system should be used for all aspects of an IT Infrastructure. It may require a process of education to convince everyone that all components of an IT Infrastructure can, and very often do, impact heavily upon each other, and that changes to individual configuration items require coordination.

Attempts may be made to implement changes without reference to the change management process. Strict disciplines should be introduced to prevent this. These should include:

* regular independent audits to check that change management staff, other IT Services staff and Users are adhering to the change management procedures described in this module (see Section 5.1.4)

* management controls over the activities of in-house and contractors' support staff, and engineers

* configuration management control of all configuration items and versions

* Help desk detection of user access to equipment or software that is unknown to the configuration management system.

It may be difficult to ensure that contractors' representatives, such as hardware engineers, adhere to the organization's change management procedures. It is recommended that contracts with suppliers should, where possible, include the need for such compliance. Condition 12 of the standard CC88 Contract, part 2-C reads:

"If the CONTRACTOR proposes to modify any part of the Contractually Maintained Hardware (CMH) the CONTRACTOR shall notify the AUTHORITY and **request the AUTHORITY's agreement** to the proposed modification, such an agreement not to be unreasonably withheld. If such an agreement is given then the modification shall be carried out at a mutually convenient time."

7. Tools

Support tools will be essential for all except the very smallest change management system. Ideally a configuration management-based tool, capable of storing all relevant configuration items (CIs), and the important relationships between them, should be used. Such a tool should have the following facilities:

*   RFCs and PRs stored upon the same database, in an easily accessible format

*   the ability to identify the relationship between RFCs, PRs and CIs

*   the ability to identify easily the other CIs that will be impacted whenever a change to any specific CI is proposed

*   automatic production of requests for impact and resources assessment to the 'owners' of the impacted CIs

*   the ability for all authorized personnel to submit RFCs from their own terminal or location

*   the ability to 'progress' requests through the appropriate stages of authorization and implementation and to maintain clear records of this progress

*   the ability to allow change management staff, change builders, testers, etc to add text to change records

*   clear definition of back-out procedures should a change cause problems

*   automatic warnings of any RFCs that exceed pre-specified time periods during any stage

*   automatic prompting to carry out reviews of implemented changes

*   automatic generation of management and trend information relating to changes

*   automatic production of change schedules.

Tools that are currently available which provide some of these facilities include IBM's INFO/MAN, CA's Netman and Softool's Change & Configuration Control Environment (CCC). Unfortunately there is no tool currently on the market that provides all the facilities, and in many operating environments no purpose built change management tools exist.

Free standing PC-based database and spreadsheet packages can, however, be used to log changes in any environment.

CCTA is working with the IT trade to improve the availability of change management support tools. Further information is available from the contact shown in section 9.

8. Conclusions and Recommendations

A comprehensive change management system to manage the initiation, implementation and review of all changes, proposed and actual, to the IT Infrastructure is essential to ensure high quality IT services to users. The main recommendation of this module is that all organizations implement such a system as quickly as practical.

Other recommendations are that:

*   logging and control of changes should be an integral part of a comprehensive configuration management system

*   support tools will be required for all except the very smallest systems

*   where no RFC format is imposed by support tools, the items as shown in Annex E should be included in the RFC form used

*   all IT Services staff must be free to submit RFCs. Consider a requirement for user requests to be signed by a User Manager, to filter out impractical RFCs or those that are not supported by the wider user community, and to collate similar requests, thus reducing volumes

*   a forward schedule of changes should be issued

*   all changes should be thoroughly tested by an independent test group, prior to implementation

*   the interval between CAB meetings should not normally exceed 20 working days, and meetings should normally last no longer than 2 hours

*   there should be a direct cut-over from existing to new change management systems, as parallel-running is impractical

*   outstanding changes should be regularly reviewed

*   changes implemented should be reviewed after a pre-defined period

*   the change management function must be regularly reviewed for efficiency and effectiveness and audited for compliance with this guidance

*   contracts with suppliers and maintainers should incorporate the requirement for the contractor's staff to comply with the organization's change management procedures.

9. Further Information

Further information on the contents of this module can be obtained from:

Information Systems Engineering Group
CCTA
Rosebery Court
St Andrews Business Park
NORWICH
NR7 0HS
Tel 01603 704704 (GTN 3040 4704)

Annex A. Glossary of Terms

Acronyms and Abbreviations Used In This Module

CAB
Change Advisory Board

CAB/EC
Change Advisory Board/Executive Committee

CCTA
Central Computer and Telecommunications Agency

CI
Configuration Item

CMH
Contractually Maintained Hardware

EIFIT
Environmental Infrastructure for Information Technology

IR
Incident Report

ITEC
IT Executive Committee

ITPS
IT Planning Secretariat

PR
Problem Report

RFC
Request for Change

Definitions

Configuration Item (CI)
A component of an IT Infrastructure, normally the smallest unit that can be changed independently of other components. CIs may vary widely in complexity, size and type - from an entire system to a single module or a minor hardware component.

Configuration Management
The process of identifying and defining the configuration items in a system, recording and reporting the status of configuration items and requests for change, and verifying the completeness and correctness of configuration items.

Incident
A single occurrence of deviation from the specification of an IT
infrastructure component or an aspect of IT service.

Incident Report (IR)
A form, or screen, containing details of incidents involving any
component of an IT Infrastructure or any aspect of the IT
service.

Problem
The underlying cause of multiple occurrences of incidents; also,
a serious incident.

Problem Report (PR)
A form, or screen, containing details of problems with any
component of an IT Infrastructure or any aspect of the IT
service.

PRINCE
The standard government method for project management.

Release
A collection of new and/or changed configuration items which
are tested and introduced into the live environment together.

Request for Change
A form or screen, used to record details of a request for a
change to any component of an IT Infrastructure or any aspect
of IT services.

Annex B. Job Description - Change Manager

Main Duties

1 Receives, logs and allocates priority, in collaboration with the initiator, to all Requests for Change (RFC). Rejects any RFCs that are totally impractical.

2 Tables all non-urgent RFCs for a Change Advisory Board (CAB) meeting, issues agenda and circulates all RFCs to CAB members in advance of meetings to allow prior consideration: convenes an urgent CAB or CAB/EC meeting for all priority 0 (urgent) RFCs.

3 Chairs all CAB and CAB/EC meetings. After consideration of the advice given by the CAB or CAB/EC, authorizes those changes that are acceptable. Issues forward schedules of changes, via the Help Desk.

4 Liaises with all necessary parties to coordinate change building, testing and implementation, in accordance with schedules. Updates change log with all progress that occurs, including any actions to correct problems and /or to take opportunities to improve IT service quality.

5 Reviews all implemented changes to ensure that they have met their objectives. Refers-back any that have been unsuccessful.

6 Reviews all outstanding RFCs awaiting consideration or awaiting action.

7 Analyses change records to determine any trends or apparent problems that occur. Seeks rectification with relevant parties.

8 Produces regular and accurate management reports.

Annex C. Sample Mission Statement for the Change Management Function

In order to clarify the objectives of the change management function, you should define a 'mission statement'. Your mission statement should describe the reason why you are implementing or improving the change management system. Documenting this will help you to ensure that other members of the organization understand your overall goal.

The mission statement given below is a sample which you may wish to use, or adapt to your own requirements.

"Ensure that standardized methods and procedures are used for efficient and prompt handling of all changes, in order to minimize the impact of change related problems upon IT service quality."

Annex D. Typical Responsibilities - CAB Member

Main Duties

1   Reviews all Requests for Change (RFC) submitted by the Change Manager. As appropriate, determines and provides details of likely impact, implementation resources, and ongoing costs of all changes.

2   Attends all relevant Change Advisory Board (CAB) meetings. Considers all changes on agenda and gives opinion on which changes should be authorized. Participates in scheduling of all changes.

3   (CAB/EC Only). Is available to be contacted should an urgent change be required. Provides advice to Change Manager on aspects of proposed urgent changes.

Annex E. Items To Be Included in an RFC Form

1	RFC Number (plus cross reference to Problem Report number where necessary).
2	Description and identity of item to be changed (including CI identification if Configuration Management System in use).
3	Reason for change.
4	Version of item to be changed.
5	Name, location and telephone number of person proposing the change.
6	Date change proposed.
7	Change priority.
8	Impact and resource assessment (may be on separate forms where convenient).
9	CAB recommendations (may be held separately with impact and resource assessments where convenient).
10	Authorization signature.
11	Authorization time/date.
12	Scheduled implementation (release identification and/or date and time).
13	Details of change builder/implementor.
14	Actual implementation time/date.
15	Review date.
16	Review results (including cross reference to new RFC where necessary).

Annex F. Example Priority Rating

The following priority ratings are provided as examples.

Priority Level	Description and Action Required
0	**Urgent:** Causing loss of service or severe usability problems to a large number of users, or some equally serious problem. Immediate action required. Urgent CAB or CAB/EC meeting to be convened. Resources to be allocated immediately to implement authorized change.
1	**High Priority:** Severely affecting some users, or impacting upon a large number of users. To be given highest priority when being considered by the CAB, and for change building, testing and implementation resources.
2	**Medium Priority:** No severe impact, but rectification cannot be deferred until next scheduled release or upgrade. To be allocated medium priority by CAB and for resources.
3	**Low Priority:** A change is justified and necessary, but can wait until the next scheduled release or upgrade. To be allocated resources accordingly.

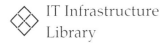

The price of this publication has been set to make some contribution to the
preparation costs incurred by the department.

Printed in the United Kingdom for The Stationery Office
J0086088 7/99 C6 10170

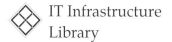

IT Infrastructure
Library

Comments Sheet
Change Management

CCTA hopes that you find this book both useful and interesting. We will welcome your comments and suggestions for improving it.
Please use this form or a photocopy, and continue on a further sheet if needed.

From:		re: **Issue 1**
Name		**April 1989**

Organization

Address

Telephone

COVERAGE
Does the material cover your needs?
If not, then what additional material would you like included.

CLARITY
Are there any points which are unclear?
If yes, please detail where and why.

ACCURACY
Please give details of any inaccuracies found.

If more space is required for these or other comments, please continue overleaf.

RECEIPT

Do you know of any other person within your
organization who would like a copy of this book?

OTHER COMMENTS

Return to: **Information Systems Engineering Group**
                 CCTA
                 Rosebery Court
                 St Andrews Business Park
                 Norwich, NR7 0HS